COUNTRY PROFILES

MOROCCO

BY ALICIA Z. KLEPEIS

BELLWETHER MEDIA • MINNEAPOLIS, MN

Blastoff! Discovery launches a new mission: reading to learn. Filled with facts and features, each book offers you an exciting new world to explore!

This edition first published in 2020 by Bellwether Media, Inc.

No part of this publication may be reproduced in whole or in part without written permission of the publisher.
For information regarding permission, write to Bellwether Media, Inc.,
Attention: Permissions Department,
6012 Blue Circle Drive, Minnetonka, MN 55343.

Library of Congress Cataloging-in-Publication Data

Names: Klepeis, Alicia, 1971- author.
Title: Morocco / by Alicia Z. Klepeis.
Description: Minneapolis, MN : Bellwether Media, Inc., 2020. |
    Series: Blastoff! Discovery: Country profiles | Includes
    bibliographical references and index. | Audience: Ages 7-13 |
    Audience: Grades 4-6 |
  Summary: "Engaging images accompany information about
    Morocco. The combination of high-interest subject matter and
    narrative text is intended for students in grades 3 through
    8"– Provided by publisher.
Identifiers: LCCN 2019034869 (print) | LCCN 2019034870 (ebook)
    | ISBN 9781644871706 (library binding) | ISBN
    9781618918468 (ebook)
Subjects: LCSH: Morocco–Juvenile literature. | Morocco–Social life
    and customs–Juvenile literature.
Classification: LCC DT305 .K57 2020 (print) | LCC DT305 (ebook)
    | DDC 964–dc23
LC record available at https://lccn.loc.gov/2019034869
LC ebook record available at https://lccn.loc.gov/2019034870

Editor: Rebecca Sabelko   Designer: Brittany McIntosh

Printed in the United States of America, North Mankato, MN.

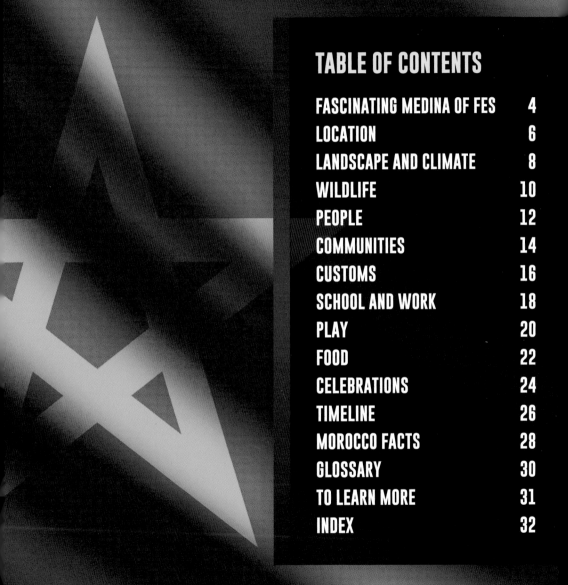

TABLE OF CONTENTS

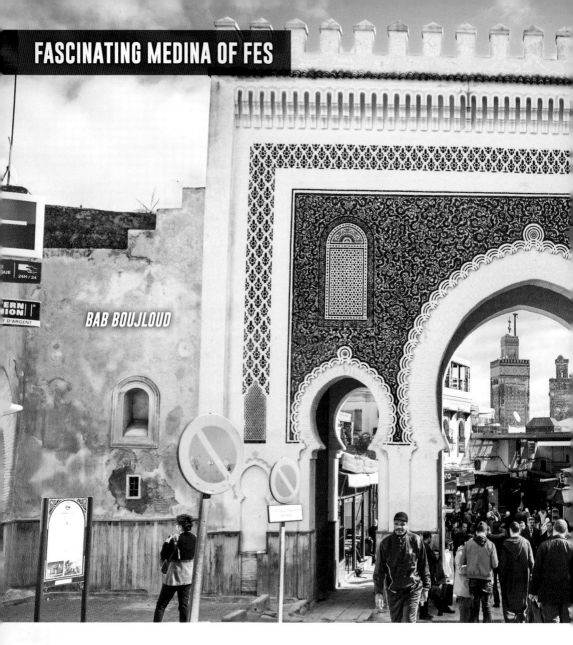

BAB BOUJLOUD

The sun is fierce as a family arrives at the centuries-old **Medina** of Fes. They meet their guide at the beautifully tiled *Bab Boujloud*, or Blue Gate of Fes. Inside, alleyways wind like a maze. The family wanders past shops selling spices, leather goods, and colorful glass lanterns.

OTHER TOP SITES

ATLAS MOUNTAINS

CHEFCHAOUEN, THE BLUE CITY

ERG CHEBBI

ESSAOUIRA BEACHES

During lunch, they sip sweet mint tea at a rooftop restaurant. They admire the stunning views of the medina. They also spot the green ceramic-tiled roofs of the University of Al-Karaouine. It dates back to 859 CE. Welcome to Morocco!

Morocco is located in North Africa. It covers 172,414 square miles (446,550 square kilometers). Rabat, the capital, lies on the Atlantic coast just north of Casablanca, Morocco's largest city.

Morocco does not have many land neighbors. Algeria lies to its east and southeast. Western Sahara borders Morocco to the south. Morocco claims Western Sahara as its own territory, but Western Sahara's **native** people disagree. Waves of the Atlantic Ocean crash upon Morocco's western shores. The Mediterranean Sea laps upon the northern coast. Two small Spanish territories, Melilla and Ceuta, are found in northern Morocco.

ATLANTIC OCEAN

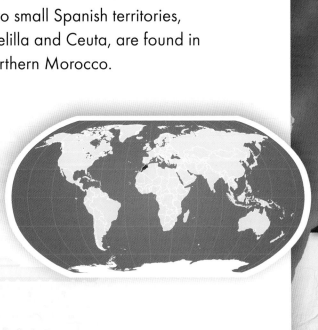

WESTERN SAHARA

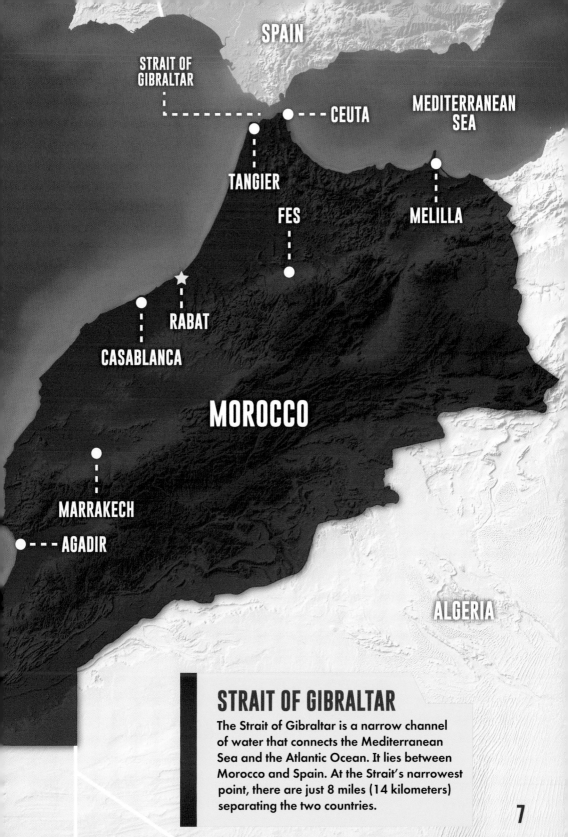

SPAIN

STRAIT OF
GIBRALTAR

MEDITERRANEAN
SEA

CEUTA

TANGIER

FES

MELILLA

RABAT

CASABLANCA

MOROCCO

MARRAKECH

AGADIR

ALGERIA

STRAIT OF GIBRALTAR

The Strait of Gibraltar is a narrow channel of water that connects the Mediterranean Sea and the Atlantic Ocean. It lies between Morocco and Spain. At the Strait's narrowest point, there are just 8 miles (14 kilometers) separating the two countries.

LANDSCAPE AND CLIMATE

= SAHARA DESERT
= ATLAS MOUNTAINS
= RIF MOUNTAINS

Most of the land in Morocco is high in **elevation**. The Rif Mountains lie in the north along the Mediterranean coastline. The Taza Gap separates the Rif from the towering Atlas Mountains that run through the center of Morocco. The **plains** of the Moroccan **Plateau** stretch between the Atlantic coast and the mountains south of Rabat and Fes. The Sahara Desert makes up Morocco's southern and southeastern sections.

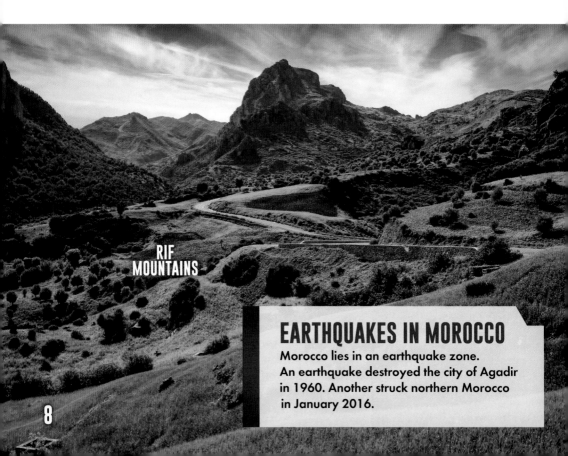

RIF MOUNTAINS

EARTHQUAKES IN MOROCCO

Morocco lies in an earthquake zone. An earthquake destroyed the city of Agadir in 1960. Another struck northern Morocco in January 2016.

SAHARA DESERT

RABAT
Average seasonal highs and lows

JANUARY
HIGH: 63 °F (17 °C)
LOW: 45 °F (7 °C)

APRIL
HIGH: 69 °F (21 °C)
LOW: 51 °F (11 °C)

JULY
HIGH: 81 °F (27 °C)
LOW: 64 °F (18 °C)

OCTOBER
HIGH: 76 °F (24 °C)
LOW: 58 °F (14 °C)

°F = degrees Fahrenheit
°C = degrees Celsius

Most of Morocco has mild, wet winters and hot, dry summers. The rainy season usually lasts from October to April. Temperatures can be much cooler in the mountains, where snow may occur.

WILDLIFE

Morocco is home to a variety of wildlife. In the Sahara, fennec foxes are on the prowl for jerboa munching on desert plants. Desert hedgehogs come out at night to avoid the heat. They root around for bird eggs, scorpions, and baby snakes.

Wild boars roam on forested mountain slopes while eagles soar above hoping to spot prey. Barbary macaques munch on fruits and fungi in the Atlas Mountains. Dolphins dive for fish along the coasts as sea birds fly overhead. **Endangered** Mediterranean monk seals feed close to the shore.

BOTTLENOSE DOLPHINS

LESSER EGYPTIAN JERBOA

BALD IBIS

FENNEC FOX

SOUSS-MASSA

Souss-Massa National Park is located on Morocco's Atlantic coast. Swallows, purple herons, and spoonbills dwell in this park. It is also where one of the last wild flocks of northern bald ibis is found!

BARBARY
MACAQUES

BARBARY MACAQUE

Life Span: 22 years
Red List Status: endangered

Barbary macaque range =

LEAST CONCERN	NEAR THREATENED	VULNERABLE	ENDANGERED	CRITICALLY ENDANGERED	EXTINCT IN THE WILD	EXTINCT

11

Over 34 million people live in Morocco. Nearly all Moroccans have backgrounds from a mixture of the **Arab** and Berber **ethnic** groups. The native Berbers have dwelled in North Africa for many centuries. Morocco is also home to a small population of Spanish and sub-Saharan African **descendants**. About 100,000 **foreign** workers live in Morocco as well.

Almost all Moroccans practice the official religion of Islam. About 1 out of 100 Moroccans are not Muslims. They may practice Christianity, Judaism, or Baha'i. Arabic and Tamazight, or Berber, are the nation's official languages. People also speak French for business and government matters.

FAMOUS FACE

Name: Nawal El Moutawakel
Birthday: April 15, 1962
Hometown: Casablanca, Morocco
Famous for: The first woman from an Islamic majority country to win an Olympic gold medal (1984) and two-time Minister of Sports in the Moroccan cabinet

SPEAK ARABIC

Arabic uses script instead of letters. However, Arabic words can be written with the English alphabet so you can read them.

ENGLISH	ARABIC	HOW TO SAY IT
hello	marhaban	mar-HAB-ah
goodbye	ma'a as-salama	ma ahs-sah-LAH-mah
please (to males)	min fadlak	min FAHD-lehck
please (to females)	min fadlik	min FAHD-lick
thank you	shukran	SHUH-krahn
yes	na'am	NAHM
no	laa	LAH-ah

CHEFCHAOUEN

COMMUNITIES

Over half of Moroccans live in **urban** areas such as Casablanca and Rabat. Most people live in apartments. But the wealthy may live in large, expensive houses. Homes in **rural** areas are often made of mud bricks. People in Casablanca often travel by **tram**, bus, or car. In the mountains, people may use donkeys for transportation. Camels help move people and goods in the deserts.

TRAM
CASABLANCA

FROM HOME TO HOTEL

Riads are traditional houses in Morocco. They have a courtyard with beautiful plants and tilework. They may even have fountains. Many riads have been turned into hotels or guest houses.

Family is important to Moroccans. It is **tradition** for women to stay home to take care of their children and manage the household. Adult children often live with their parents until they get married.

People in Morocco are known for being warm and affectionate. They greet others with a phrase that means "May peace be upon you." People of the same gender may greet one another with a hug or kiss on the cheek.

In Morocco's cities, people often wear the same kinds of clothes seen in New York or London. However, shorts are something Moroccans only wear at the beach. Traditional Moroccan clothing is colorful. It may feature beautiful embroidery. The *djellaba* is a popular ankle-length garment worn across the country. It has long sleeves and a hood.

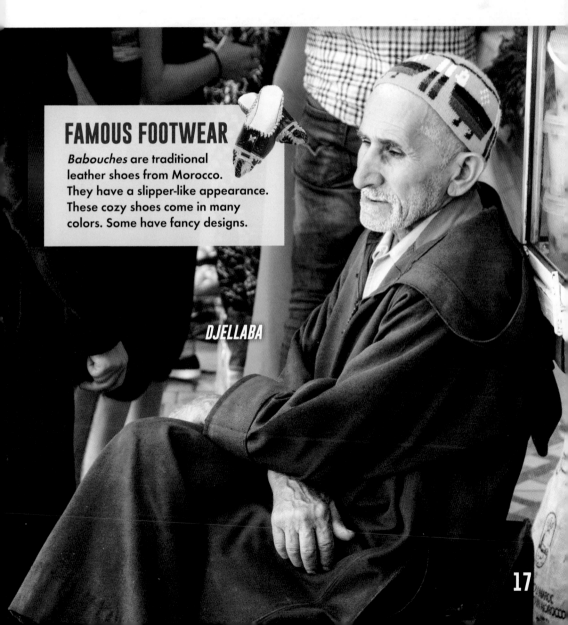

FAMOUS FOOTWEAR

Babouches are traditional leather shoes from Morocco. They have a slipper-like appearance. These cozy shoes come in many colors. Some have fancy designs.

DJELLABA

Students in Morocco begin primary school at age 6. After six years of primary school, children are required to attend three years of secondary school. Some students are not able to complete their education. But the number of students attending high school is growing.

About 4 out of 10 Moroccans have **service jobs**. Some people work in the **tourism** industry. Others have jobs in banks or the government. Moroccan workers also **manufacture** products such as clothing, leather goods, and chemicals. Farmers grow citrus fruits, grains, cotton, and sugarcane. They also raise livestock including cattle and sheep.

CAMEL TOUR

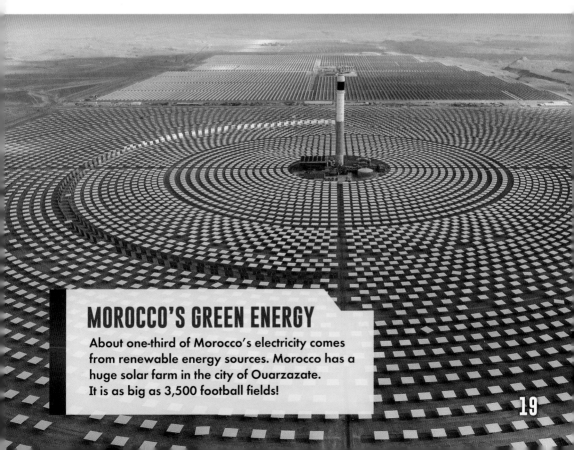

MOROCCO'S GREEN ENERGY

About one-third of Morocco's electricity comes from renewable energy sources. Morocco has a huge solar farm in the city of Ouarzazate. It is as big as 3,500 football fields!

19

SOCCER

Soccer is the most popular sport in Morocco. The young and old participate in matches. Tennis and golf are growing in popularity. Moroccan athletes have been quite successful in track and field as well. People can ski and snowboard in the Atlas Mountains. Camel and horseback riding are popular traditional activities.

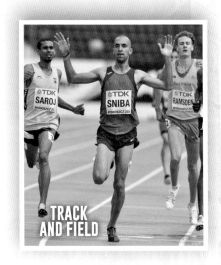

TRACK AND FIELD

Moroccans enjoy spending free time visiting with family and friends. Men may socialize in cafes. Some play chess or cards. Others chat about sports or politics. Young women commonly meet up to go shopping. Women also catch up over tea in their homes.

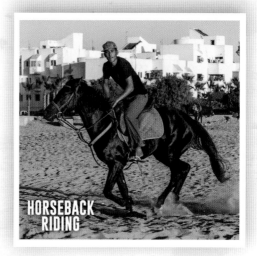

HORSEBACK RIDING

HENNA HANDS

Moroccans sometimes decorate their hands and feet with henna for special events such as weddings. Try creating your own designs!

What You Need:
- construction paper
- scissors
- a pencil
- black and brown markers

Instructions:

1. Look at some photos online of henna designs that people in Morocco wear on their hands. In northern Morocco, floral designs are common. In the southern areas, bigger and bolder designs are well-liked.

2. Trace each of your hands onto the construction paper. Trace just past your wrist. It may be helpful to have your fingers stretched slightly apart.

3. Use your scissors to cut out the tracings of each of your hands.

4. Use your black and brown markers to create "henna" designs on each of the paper hand cutouts.

5. When you are happy with the result, display your decorated hands. Trace and cut out feet designs to decorate next!

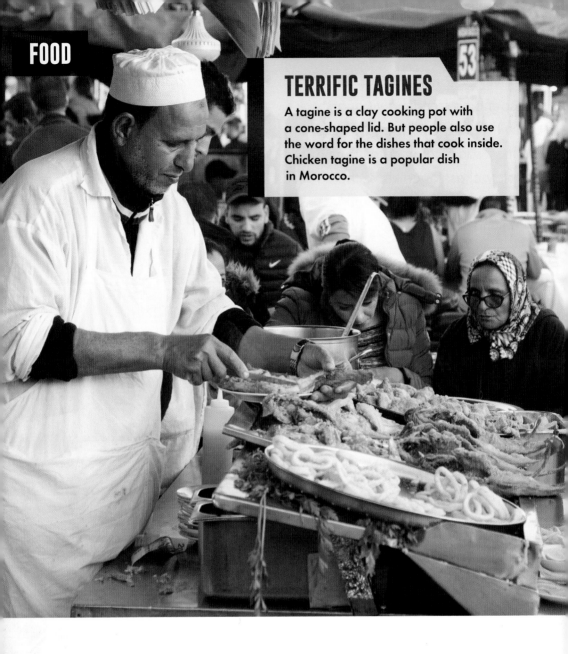

TERRIFIC TAGINES

A tagine is a clay cooking pot with a cone-shaped lid. But people also use the word for the dishes that cook inside. Chicken tagine is a popular dish in Morocco.

Moroccans cook with many spices. These include cumin, coriander, and cinnamon. Bread, fish, and lamb are **staples** in Morocco. Couscous, the national dish, is served with vegetables and a meat sauce. People also enjoy fruits of all kinds.

A traditional soup called *B'ssara* is often eaten for breakfast. It is made of beans, olive oil, and cumin. The biggest meal of the day is lunch. People often eat salads or soups at the beginning of the meal. *Harira* is a soup made with tomatoes, chickpeas, lentils, and lamb. People often enjoy nuts, fruits, and pastries for dessert.

HARIRA

COUSCOUS

ORANGE MESKOUTA

Meskouta is a traditional cake from Morocco.

Ingredients:
zest and juice of one orange
4 eggs
1 1/2 cups sugar
1/2 cup vegetable oil
2 cups flour
4 teaspoons baking powder
1/4 teaspoon salt
1 1/4 teaspoons vanilla extract

Steps:
1. With an adult present, preheat the oven to 350 degrees Fahrenheit (177 degrees Celsius). Grease your pan, then sprinkle some flour on top.

2. Grate the orange zest. Add this into the orange juice.

3. In a large bowl, combine eggs and sugar. Slowly add in the oil. Then add flour, baking powder, and salt.

4. Add the orange juice, zest, and vanilla. Pour the batter into the pan.

5. Bake for 35-45 minutes. Let the cake cool and enjoy!

Like many countries, Morocco celebrates New Year's Day on January 1. But later in January, the Berber community celebrates its own new year called *Yennayer*. They dance, sing, and make couscous as they celebrate and wish for a good farming year ahead. November 18 is Independence Day. Parades and political speeches take place.

Many of Morocco's biggest celebrations are Muslim holidays. *Eid al-Fitr* marks the end of the holy month of Ramadan. Moroccans have feasts and offer gifts to the poor. Moroccans celebrate their **culture** and country all year long!

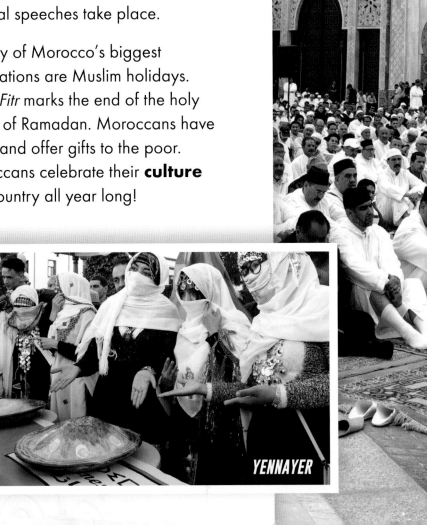

YENNAYER

THE DATES FESTIVAL

Erfoud is a town in the Sahara Desert. It hosts the Dates Festival each October. People dance, sing, and parade through town wearing traditional costumes to celebrate the harvest. There are also camel races.

EID AL-FITR

LATE 600s
Arabs invade the region and introduce Islam

40 CE
Morocco and surrounding areas are controlled by the Roman Empire

1912
Morocco is under the control of France with Spain having control over coastal areas

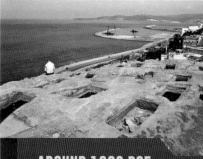

LATE 1700s
Morocco becomes known as an Islamic monarchy

AROUND 1200 BCE
Phoenician traders set up storage areas along Morocco's coast

1956
Morocco gains independence from France

1976
Morocco and Mauritania divide the territory of Western Sahara

2004
A powerful earthquake strikes northern Morocco

2018
Morocco accuses Iran of supplying weapons and training to independence fighters in Western Sahara

1999
Mohammed VI becomes Morocco's new king

Official Name: Kingdom of Morocco

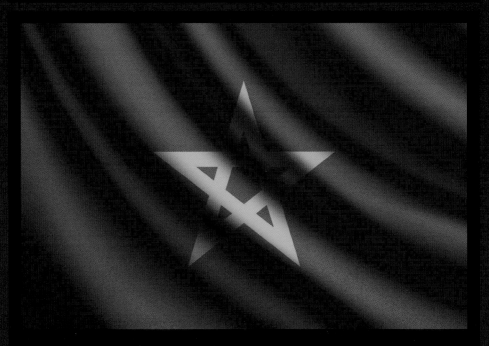

Flag of Morocco: Morocco's flag is red with a green star in the middle. The five-pointed star is called a pentacle. It represents the five pillars of Islam, duties required of all Muslim people. Both red and green are traditional colors in Arab flags. The flag's red background represents bravery and strength. Green stands for love, peace, and hope. Green is also the color of Islam.

Area: 172,414 square miles
(446,550 square kilometers)

Capital City: Rabat

Important Cities: Casablanca, Fes, Tangier, Marrakech, Agadir

Population:
34,314,130 (July 2018)

WHERE PEOPLE LIVE

COUNTRYSIDE 37%

CITY 63%

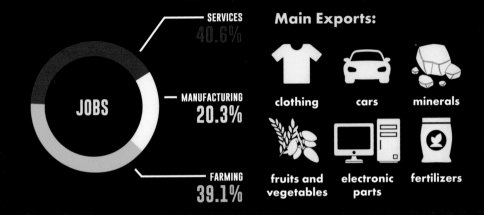

SERVICES
40.6%

JOBS

MANUFACTURING
20.3%

FARMING
39.1%

Main Exports:

clothing

cars

minerals

fruits and vegetables

electronic parts

fertilizers

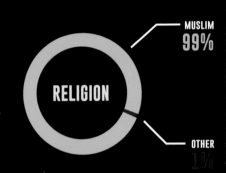

National Holiday:
Throne Day (July 30)

Main Languages:
Arabic and Tamazight (Berber)

Form of Government:
parliamentary constitutional monarchy

Title for Country Leaders:
king (head of state),
prime minister (head of government)

MUSLIM
99%

RELIGION

OTHER
1%

Unit of Money:
Moroccan dirham

29

GLOSSARY

Arab—related to people who are originally from the Arabian Peninsula and who now live mostly in the Middle East and northern Africa

culture—the beliefs, arts, and ways of life in a place or society

descendants—people related to a person or group of people who lived at an earlier time

elevation—the height above sea level

endangered—at risk of becoming extinct

ethnic—related to a group of people who share customs and an identity

foreign—coming from another country

manufacture—to make products, often with machines

medina—the old Arab, non-European, section of a northern African city

native—originally from the area or related to a group of people that began in the area

plains—large areas of flat land

plateau—an area of flat, raised land

rural—related to the countryside

service jobs—jobs that perform tasks for people or businesses

staples—widely used foods or other items

tourism—the business of people traveling to visit other places

tradition—a custom, idea, or belief handed down from one generation to the next

tram—a vehicle that runs on a track or rails that is used to carry groups of people

urban—related to cities and city life

TO LEARN MORE

AT THE LIBRARY

Blauer, Ettagale, and Jason Lauré. *Morocco*. New York, N.Y.: Children's Press, 2016.

Markovics, Joyce. *Morocco*. New York, N.Y.: Bearport Publishing, 2020.

Perritano, John. *Morocco*. New York, N.Y.: AV2 by Weigl, 2019.

ON THE WEB

FACTSURFER

Factsurfer.com gives you a safe, fun way to find more information.

1. Go to www.factsurfer.com.

2. Enter "Morocco" into the search box and click Q.

3. Select your book cover to see a list of related web sites.

INDEX